KNIGHTS

FACTS ● THINGS TO MAKE ● ACTIVITIES

RACHEL WRIGHT

Franklin Watts

New York ● London ● Toronto ● Sydney

© Franklin Watts 1991

Franklin Watts
A Division of Grolier Publishing
Sherman Turnpike
Danbury, CT 06816

Library of Congress Cataloging-in-Publication Data

Wright, Rachel.
    Knights / Rachel Wright,
        p. cm. -- (Craft topics)
    Includes index,
    Summary: Introduces the characteristics and behavior of medieval
knights through a variety of crafts.
    ISBN 0-531-14163-2
    1. Handicraft--Juvenile literature. 2. Knights and knighthood-
-Juvenile literature. [1. Knights and knighthood. 2. Handicraft.]
I. Title. II. Series.
TT160.W74 1992
745.5--dc20

                                      91-20063
                                      CIP   AC

Editor: Hazel Poole
Text consultant: I. D. D. Eaves,
Keeper of Armour,
Royal Armouries,
HM Tower of London
Designed by: Sally Boothroyd
Artwork by: Ed Dovey

Printed in the United Kingdom

CONTENTS

Early Knights

Knights were armored warriors, trained to fight on horseback. For much of the Middle Ages they dominated European life, both on and off the battlefield.

The Middle Ages is the name given to the period from about the 700s AD to 1500 AD. During this time Europe was often at war. Before mounted warriors arrived on the scene, most of the fighting had been done by untrained foot soldiers. Up until then, it had been very difficult for a horseman to stay in the saddle and fight at the same time.

Between the late 700s and the 1100s, however, all this changed as western Europe saw four "inventions" come into general use. They were the stirrup, the nailed horseshoe, the high-backed saddle and the heavier lance. Together, they turned the horseman into a formidable fighting force.

▲ A 12th century picture showing knights in shock combat.

With a steel-tipped wooden lance gripped firmly under his arm, and his body held to his horse by saddle and stirrups, a rider could hit his enemy with the full force of both himself and his charging horse — all without losing his balance. The age of the knight had begun.

KNIGHT KEEPING

Kings needed knights, but they couldn't afford to keep permanent armies of them. Providing for such an army in peacetime would have cost a small fortune. So, instead of paying wages, some kings agreed to give part of their land to their leading knights. In return, these knights had to promise to be loyal, to help the king fight his wars, and to keep law and order in their own parts of the country.

These leading knights then shared out their land among their own knightly followers, offering them a similar deal. In this way, high and low knights alike had land to live on and had control over the peasants who worked on that land. This whole arrangement — land for services — was later called feudalism. It turned many knights into wealthy and powerful mini rulers.

KING

BARONS

KNIGHTS

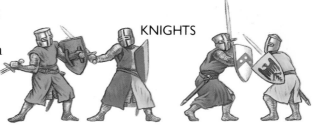

PEASANTS

Not all knights benefited from feudalism. Some remained landless, fighting for whomever would pay them. Others wandered the countryside in search of fame and fortune.

▲ This pyramid shows how feudalism was structured. Everyone was expected to serve God and their social superiors. The workers on the bottom row had the roughest deal of all. Some of them were actually owned by their overlord.

KNIGHTS OF GOD

The first knights were not necessarily nobles. They were simply men who could afford a horse. On the whole, they were rough and ready characters who earned a living by fighting. If there was no enemy about, they fought among themselves to show off their skills.

Their wild, unruly behavior began to worry the Church. In those days, the Catholic Church was immensely powerful in Europe. So, when it pointed out that knights everywhere had a duty to fight for God, protect the poor and generally start behaving themselves, many of them began to shape up.

CHIVALRY

During the 1100s, the knights went one step further and developed their own code of behavior, which the Church then sponsored. This code of behavior, called chivalry, demanded that a knight be a gentleman, uphold the law, and protect the Church, women, and orphans. Later on, it also expected the perfect knight to fight on behalf of a lady, as this was supposed to inspire him to greater bravery.

Needless to say, all this was more easily said than done, and some knights did not live up to the chivalrous ideal.

Chivalry and the Church's backing made knighthood glamorous — an honor valued by lords and kings. As a result, knights became a part of the nobility, a class of warrior aristocrats. Snobbery set in and, before long, most new knights were the sons of knights rather than of poor men.

A young lady offers her heart to the knight she has chosen as her champion. ▼

BRASS PORTRAITS

Detailed engravings of knights in armor can sometimes be found in Old European churches. These portraits were carefully engraved onto a sheet of metal, very similar to brass.

The portraits were usually made to honor someone famous who had died. They were often set in gravestones on the church floor or on top of raised tombs.

The brass shown here commemorates Sir John D'Abernoun who died in 1327. It is possibly the oldest brass in Britain and can be found in the church at Stoke D'Abernon, Surrey, England. The engraver who made it must have been highly skilled as each link of Sir John's armor is accurately shown.

The crayon copy of this brass shown on the left was made by covering the brass with a sheet of brass rubbing paper, securing the paper with masking tape, and then rubbing a brass rubbing wax crayon over the paper until the image of Sir John appeared. You can use this technique to make rubbings of all sorts of textured objects.

DRESSED TO KILL

After the first thunderous charge into battle, a knight's lance was useless. So he dropped it and fought with his main weapon, his sword. During the second half of the 1300s, however, it became common for a knight to carry a short axe or mace (knobbed or spiked club) as well.

CHAIN MAIL AND SHIELDS

The first knights wore hauberks — long shirts made from small, interlinking metal rings. They also wore open-faced iron helmets, and carried round shields.

By 1100, mounted knights were carrying kite-shaped shields, which protected their legs much better than the round shields had done.

By the 1200s, a knight bound for battle would have been dressed as shown opposite.

▲ *This 13th century picture shows three knightly weapons in action — the sword, the axe and the mace. The worried looking man on the left is trying to fire a giant catapult called a trebuchet.*

padded cap

fabric shirt

aketon
(This was a padded
coat which stopped
the hauberk from
bruising the
knight's skin.)

breeches
(Linen or
woolen stockings
were worn
underneath these.)

coif

Great helm
(This would have
been hot and
heavy to wear.)

heater shield

mail leggings
(They were attached
by laces to a belt.)

hauberk
(Rusty hauberks were
cleaned by being
tossed about in
a bag containing
sand and vinegar.)

linen (or other
fabric) surcoat
(A surcoat helped
to keep the knight
cool when fighting
in the sun.)

mail mittens
(These were
usually part
of the hauberk's
sleeves.)

Although knights kept their armor
spotless, they weren't so eager to keep
themselves clean. Until the 1200s, most
of them didn't bathe because they
thought it sapped their strength.

spurs

Plate Armor

By 1300, armor makers had learned to reinforce parts of mail armor with iron plates. By 1400, they had perfected this technique and were putting together complete suits of made-to-measure steel plated armor. Made of about 200 plates which were joined together to make 12 or more main pieces, this armor was often strapped or laced to a knight's body.

A knight certainly welcomed his squire's help when putting on his armor. ▼

The steel plates used were skillfully shaped in such a way that weapons would skid off them.

Arranged rather like a lobster shell, most of these plates overlapped each other in order to leave as few gaps as possible. Since the plates were joined to each other by smaller plates, held together by sliding rivets, the armor was fairly easy to move in. Where there had to be gaps to allow for even more movement, a knight was protected by the mail he wore underneath.

In all, a suit of plate armor, called a harness, weighed about 40 to 60 pounds. Yet, because this weight was spread evenly over a knight's body, it wasn't unbearable. In fact, one French knight proved the point by leaping onto a horse, turning a somersault and climbing the underside of a ladder — all in full armor!

Make a Knight's Helmet

You will need: stiff paper or thin cardboard • scissors or a craft knife • glue • tape • paint • paintbrush • pencil • colored paper.

3. Paint your helmet and tape it together at the back.

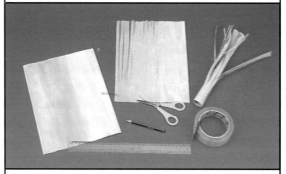

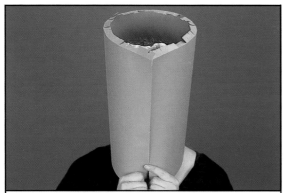

▲ **1.** Cut out a piece of stiff paper that will fit around your head. Cut and fold tabs along the top.

▲ **4.** To make a plume, draw a line across a sheet of colored paper, about 2½ inches from one edge. Cut strips up to this line. Roll the paper into a tube and tape it together.

5. Cut out a stiff paper circle for the top of your helmet and paint it. Make a hole in its center, push the plume through and secure it with tape.

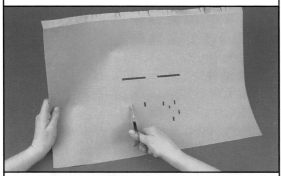

▲ **2.** Hold the paper against your face and mark two slits for your eyes. Cut these eye slits out. Don't forget to cut breathing holes too!

6. Now glue your helmet together and prepare for battle!

Although this home made helmet looks better with a plume, knights of old would have worn this type of helmet without one.

COATS OF ARMS

Chief

Fess

In the heat of battle, one knight in mail looked very like another. Therefore, to make it easier to tell friend from foe, knights had their own personal patterns or emblems painted onto their shields. These emblems, which were sometimes embroidered onto their surcoats, became known as "coats of arms."

Before long, many rich families had their own individual coat of arms, which was passed down from parent to child. Women displayed their father's or husband's arms on their personal possessions, and many wives combined the two, creating a new coat of arms.

Pale

The surface of a knight's shield was called the field. The figures or shapes on it were called charges. The simplest charges were chief, fess, pale, bar, bend, saltire, chevron, pile, cross.

Bar

The field and charges had to be painted in certain colors. Only red, black, blue, green, purple, gold and silver were allowed.

Furs, patterns which looked like animal skins or tails, were also used. The two most common ones were vair and ermine.

Bend

To ensure that each design was easy to identify, color was never placed on color; nor metal on metal; nor fur on fur.

Saltire

You may be able to find coats of arms in different places, such as school crests and stained-glass windows.

Chevron

Pile

▲ A husband's and wife's shields were sometimes combined like this, to create a new coat of arms.

▲ These shields were drawn in about 1244 by Matthew Paris. He was a learned monk and historian from St. Albans, England.

Cross

Vair

Ermine

Make a Stained-Glass Window

Design a coat of arms for you and your family. Your charges could show what your mom and dad do, or what your own hobbies are. Keep your design fairly simple as you need crayons for this project and they are not good for drawing tiny details.

You will need: white paper • a pencil • crayons • cotton balls • vegetable oil.

▲ **3.** Pour a little vegetable oil onto a cotton ball and wipe it over the back of your design.

4. When the paper is dry, tape it on a windowpane. Your coat of arms will glow when the sun shines through it, just like a stained-glass window.

▲ **1.** Draw your design on a piece of white paper and then go over its outlines in black crayon. You'll need to press quite hard.

2. Color the spaces between the black lines. Make sure that the paper shows through only where you particularly want it to.

13

PAGES AND SQUIRES

The first knighting ceremonies were very simple. After serving an apprenticeship, a would-be knight was awarded his sword and spurs by an older knight, and that was that. In time, however, both the training and the ceremony became much more complicated.

A boy of noble birth, destined to become a knight, left home at the age of 7. He was sent to a great lord's castle where he became a page, and was taught to handle horses and weapons and to be polite. In return, he had to run errands.

▲ *A quintain was used for lance practice. The squire had to hit the shield on the crossbar and duck before the sandbag on the other end of the crossbar swung around and hit him.*

When he was about 14 years old, a page became a squire. This meant that he was now the personal servant of a knight.

A squire had to take care of his master and follow him wherever he went — even into battle. If a knight got into difficulties on the battlefield, his squire came to his rescue. If he got hurt, his squire helped him to safety and dressed his wounds. If he was killed, his squire made sure that he was buried properly.

Away from the battlefield, a squire spent hours getting used to wearing armor and improving his fighting skills.

A squire's life wasn't all war and chores, though. He practiced other important knightly pursuits, such as singing, dancing and entertaining the ladies.

When he was about 18, a squire who could afford his own armor and horse was ready to become a knight. In preparation he had to have a bath, to wash away his sins. After bathing, he put on clean clothes — a red robe, to signify the blood he would shed for God, and black stockings, to remind him of death. He then spent the night praying in a castle's chapel.

His moment of glory came the next day when, after a church service, he joined other squires gathered outside. In front of an excited crowd, he stepped forward to receive his sword and golden spurs. He then knelt before a senior knight who solemnly tapped him with a sword on the neck or shoulders. At last, his years of training were over. He had become a knight.

Sometimes a squire showed such bravery in war that he was knighted on the battlefield. ▼

FIGHTING FOR FUN

Knights still practiced their skill during peacetime, playing war games. By 1100, mock battles, called tournaments or tourneys, were popular in most parts of northern Europe. Two teams of knights would spend an afternoon battering each other. The winners were those left upright at the end of the game!

As in a real war, knights tried to capture their opponents rather than kill them. Successful knights did well from the ransoms paid for captured opponents.

RULES AND REFEREES

The early tourneys had few rules and no referees. They were more like riots than sport, with players getting hurt and killed.

Later tourneys were slightly more civilized. Rules, referees and blunt weapons were introduced, and the war games themselves became part of a great carnival of chivalry.

BANS

Although tourneys were excellent training for war, the Church was shocked by their brutality and repeatedly tried to ban them. Various governments tried to curb them too, because they encouraged scheming rebels to gather in force. Yet, despite such fierce opposition, the knights refused to give way and continued fighting each other for fun.

BATTLE FOR TWO

Mock battles were popular, but jousting became even more so. The joust was a contest between two mounted knights, armed with lances. Each knight had to try to break his lance against his opponent, without hitting him below the belt. Sometimes the knights would finish their fight on foot, using either swords or poleaxes.

GAMES OF WAR

If there was a lull in a battle or a boring wait during a siege, knights from the two opposing armies might meet for a tourney. Once their game was over, they would return to their respective camps and wait for the real war to start again.

► A scene from a joust at St. Inglevert in France, taken from a 15th century copy of a chronicle about tourneying.

STAGE YOUR OWN JOUST

You will need: a large cardboard box • thick cardboard • scissors (you may prefer to use a craft knife when cutting the box and thick cardboard) • paints • paintbrushes • two smaller cardboard boxes • tissue paper • ruler • thin cardboard • foil candy wrappers • glue • pencil.

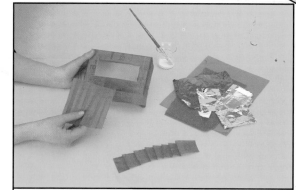

▲ **3.** Cover the stand with tissue paper. Make drapes by pleating strips of tissue paper and gluing them into position. Decorate the drapes with the foil candy wrappers.

4. Paint spectators on some thin cardboard. Cut them out and glue them to the inside of the stand's window.

5. Add thin cardboard supports, painted to look like wood, and glue the completed stand into place. Make more stands in the same way.

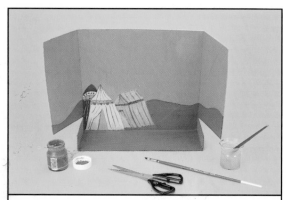

▲ **1.** Turn a large cardboard box onto one of its sides and cut away the top. Make deep cuts into the two remaining sides so that they open out slightly. Now paint the inside of the box.

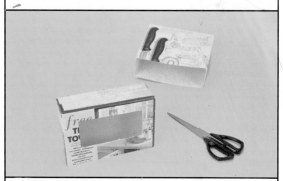

▲ **2.** To build a stand, cut a smaller box down to the size you want it. Stand it on its cut-away end and make a window in the front.

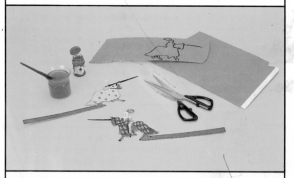

▲ **6.** Draw and then paint a charging knight on thick cardboard. Cut him out, leaving a long strip attached to his horse's back legs. Now make a second knight riding in the opposite direction.

▲ **7.** Cut a narrow slit into each side of your painted box and slot the knights into them.

▲ **8.** To avoid collisions, jousters in the second half of the 1400s were separated by a wooden barrier called a tilt.

To make a tilt, cut a strip of thick cardboard, slightly longer than the width of your box. Paint it and add a tab to each end. Coat the tabs with glue and stick the tilt between the knights.

HOLY WARS

In 1095, the Catholic Church made a dramatic plea, calling on knights everywhere to defend their Christian faith.

A group of Muslims had seized Jerusalem and were stopping Christians from visiting the city. As Jesus had lived in and around Jerusalem, Christians saw these areas as their Holy Land and wanted everybody else out.

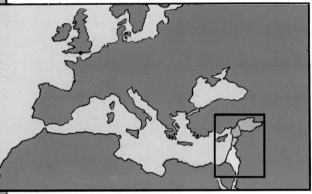

HEADING FOR THE HOLY LAND

Knights quickly rallied to the Church's call and set off on the first of their crusades. "Crusade" simply means "war of the cross." Once in the Holy Land, the crusaders fought furiously and captured Jerusalem. They set up four states of their own and built huge castles to protect themselves. However, keeping the Muslims at bay was hard work, which is why, during the 1100s, new knightly orders were founded to defend the crusading states.

◄ *Crusaders occasionally used their enemies' severed heads as missiles.*

KNIGHTS OF FAITH

The Templars, the Knights of St. John, and the Teutonic Knights were the three most important new orders. Their members were disciplined fighters who had vowed to live simply, worship God, and remain unmarried. The only trouble was that as each order grew richer, some members conveniently forgot their vows!

The three main military orders set up to defend the Holy Land at the time of the crusades. ▶

The Templars (c.1170)

The Knights of St. John (c.1250)

The Teutonic Knights (c.1280)

The Order of Teutonic Knights was set up in 1190. The Order was German in origin and its early work involved helping German pilgrims in the Holy Land.

Krak des Chevaliers, in Syria. Crusaders also learned something about castle-building from the Arabs. ▶

Feared and envied by European rulers, many Templars were burned to death after the crusades, and in 1313 their order was disbanded. The other orders fared better, and ended up doing their Christian work both in Europe and abroad.

Yet, in spite of their failings, it was largely due to these orders that the Christians managed to hold on to the Holy Land until 1291.

RICHES FROM THE EAST

Many crusaders profited from their stay in the Holy Land. They learned how to make paper, windmills and carpets. They later returned to Europe armed with silks, velvets, dyes, mirrors, apricots, rice and melons, as well as new ideas about astronomy and math. If nothing else, the crusades gave knights knowledge and luxuries they had not known before.

The Templars were founded in the early 1100s. Their job was to care for pilgrims and to protect the Holy Sepulcher where Jesus was buried.

The main mission of the Order of St. John was to care for poor and sick pilgrims visiting the Holy Land. It became a military Order at the time of the first crusades in the early 1100s.

Fortress Homes

Few knights owned castles, but many lived in them.

Sticks and Stones

The first castles were made of wood. They were later replaced by much larger stone castles, surrounded by thick stone walls. These new castles were like tiny towns, with tailors, priests and bakers all working within their walls.

Under Attack

Castles were fortresses as well as homes. Where possible, they were built on or near natural defenses such as hills and rivers. Even so, an uninvited army could still force its way into them.

Attackers sometimes tried to starve their enemy into surrender by camping outside the castle and stopping all food deliveries. This was called mounting a siege. However, if the castle was well-stocked, a siege could drag on for months. This deterred many attackers who couldn't afford to leave their own homes unguarded for so long.

Those who preferred a quicker form of attack often tried to storm their way in instead. Using giant catapults, they hurled rocks at or over the castle walls, and tried to smash down the gate with a battering ram.

While these assaults were going on above ground, fellow attackers might be busy tunneling beneath the castle walls. When they had finished, they burned the wooden props used to support the tunnel's roof and waited for the wall to collapse.

Some knights refused to dirty their hands tunneling and only took part in hand-to-hand combat. They considered all other forms of warfare most unknightly!

Climbing the Walls

Attackers often tried to take a castle by direct assault, too. Dodging arrows, rocks and boiling water or oil fired down from above, they would rush to scale the walls. Some would use ladders, while others climbed tall wooden siege towers which were wheeled up against the castle wall.

The catapults to the left of the castle are trebuchets. The catapult with a spoonlike arm is a mangonel. Both could hurl heavy missiles, but the trubuchet was the more accurate of the two. ▼

SUPER CASTLES

As the Middle Ages progressed, European castles gradually improved. More outer walls were added, moats were dug to stop tunneling, and gatehouses were built to defend the castle's entrance. Until the 1400s, when cannons became popular, these castles were almost impossible to attack successfully.

▲ Caerphilly Castle, Wales.

CARDBOARD CASTLES

The main tower of the early stone castles was called the keep. This was where the castle's lord and his knights ate and slept.

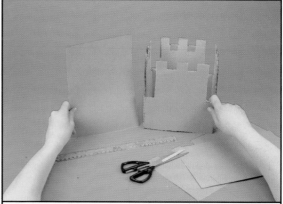

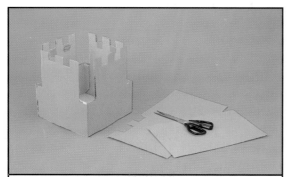

TO MAKE A KEEP

▲ **1.** Cut evenly spaced notches along the top of a large square cardboard box. Cut deeper notches at each corner and cover the box with cardboard.

▲ *Rochester Castle, Kent, England*

TO MAKE A TOWER FOR THE KEEP

▲ **2.** Cut out a piece of cardboard. It should be slightly taller than the keep, but the same width.

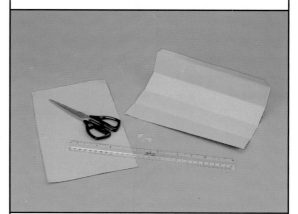

▲ **3.** Fold the cardboard lengthwise into four with a tab at one end. Open it out again.

4. Cut arrow slits into the two center panels so that castle defenders can fire out, but enemy archers can't shoot in.

5. Make battlements by cutting evenly spaced notches along the top of the tower. Use a craft knife to cut arrow slits into the higher parts of your battlements.

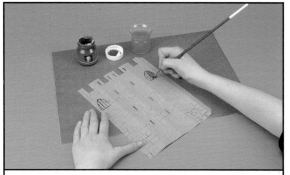

▲ **6.** Decorate the tower and paint doors near the top of each of its outer panels. Check that the base of each door starts below the keep's battlements, when the tower is in place.

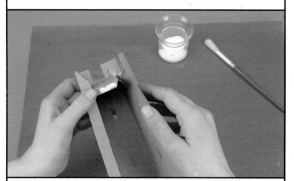

TO MAKE THE TOWER'S ROOF

▲ **7.** Measure the width of one of your tower's panels. Draw a square with sides this same length.

8. Paint the square, add four tabs and cut out the whole shape.

▲ **9.** Cover all four tabs with glue and fold the tower around its roof. Now glue the side of the tower.

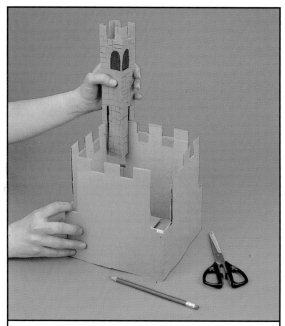

▲ **10.** Rest the tower on a corner of the keep, with its glued panels facing inward. Mark the tower where it touches the keep. Using these marks as guidelines, make two long cuts and slot the tower into place. If the tower looks crooked, trim the bottom of its two inner panels.

11. Make three more towers for your keep in the same way.

12. Finally, glue a paper flag onto four shortened straws and glue the straws to each tower's roof.

Stone keeps had rampart walks so that their soldiers could get from one tower to another.

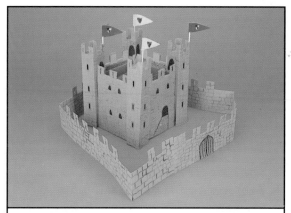

TO MAKE RAMPART WALKS

13. Cut out a rectangle of cardboard, long enough to fit between two towers.

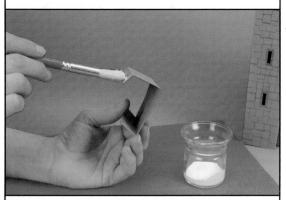

▲ **14.** Fold the cardboard as shown and and cover the two tabs with glue.

TO MAKE CURTAIN WALLS

▲ **17.** Cut notches along the top of painted strips of cardboard. Don't forget to cut arrow slits, too. Position the strips around your keep, gluing them together where necessary. Where your wall bends into a corner, cut off a couple of the notches.

▲ **15.** Stick the two tabs to the keep, just below the battlements. Repeat this until you have four walkways joining your towers.

16. When your keep and walkways are complete, paint them.

▲ **18.** Make wall towers in the same way that you made the towers for your keep and slot them into the corners of your curtain wall. Glue rampart walks to each wall.

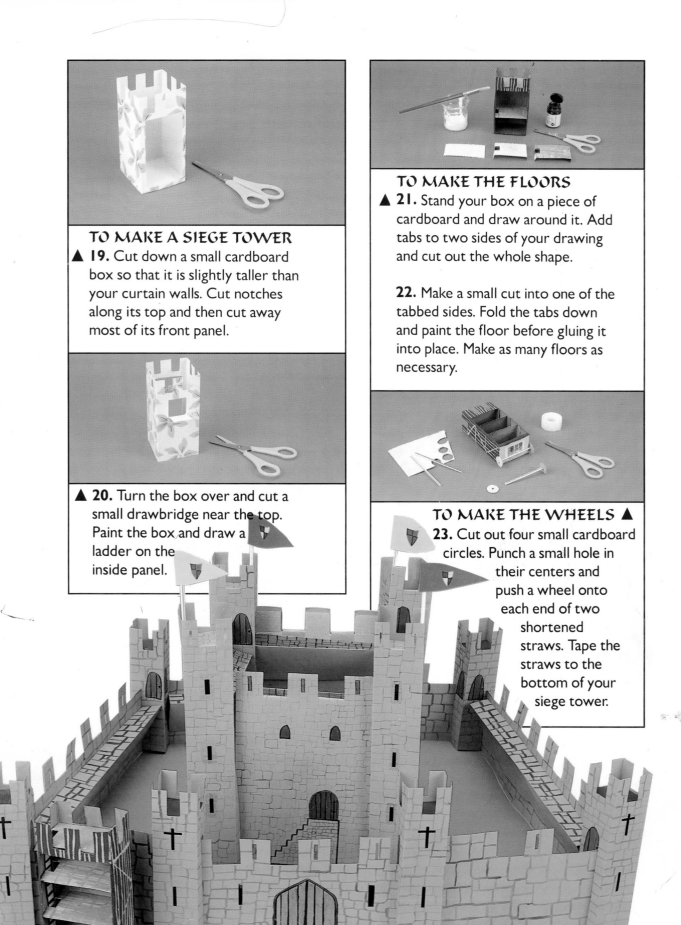

TO MAKE A SIEGE TOWER

▲ **19.** Cut down a small cardboard box so that it is slightly taller than your curtain walls. Cut notches along its top and then cut away most of its front panel.

▲ **20.** Turn the box over and cut a small drawbridge near the top. Paint the box and draw a ladder on the inside panel.

TO MAKE THE FLOORS

▲ **21.** Stand your box on a piece of cardboard and draw around it. Add tabs to two sides of your drawing and cut out the whole shape.

22. Make a small cut into one of the tabbed sides. Fold the tabs down and paint the floor before gluing it into place. Make as many floors as necessary.

TO MAKE THE WHEELS ▲

23. Cut out four small cardboard circles. Punch a small hole in their centers and push a wheel onto each end of two shortened straws. Tape the straws to the bottom of your siege tower.

Knightly Frieze

The Bayeux Tapestry is probably the most famous piece of embroidery in the world. Two hundred and thirty feet long, it shows the events leading up to William the Conqueror's invasion of England in 1066.

Using the Bayeux Tapestry for inspiration, why not make a fabric frieze? It could show a day in the life of a knight or the story of a spectacular battle.

1. To make your cloth background very firm, glue a piece of thick cardboard onto the back of your length of material.

2. Draw your designs on tracing paper and trace them onto some fabric. Cut out your fabric shapes and arrange them on a cloth background before gluing them down.

You will need: tracing paper • a pencil • a length of rayon or calico for the background • a piece of thick cardboard • sharp scissors • white glue • glue brush • toothpicks for spreading tiny amounts of glue • fabric scraps • ribbons • yarns • threads • sequins, etc.

3. Try fraying, pleating, braiding, and overlapping fabrics to create different effects. Add extra detail using ribbon, thread, buttons and beads.

THE END OF THE KNIGHT

By the 1200s, feudalism had started to crumble and leading knights no longer had to fight for the king. Instead, they gave him money to hire soldiers to take their place.

The times were gradually changing in other ways, too. Europe started to become more peaceful, and trade began to boom. Successful merchants and traders found that they could now buy their way into the nobility. The knightly class was no longer as select as it had once been.

FOOTMEN VERSUS CAVALRYMEN

Things were looking bad for knights . . . and getting worse. By the 1500s, longbows, handguns and cannons had all become common weaponry, and the old-fashioned knight was clearly no match for any of them.

Foot soldiers, called pikemen, had also arrived to stay. Standing in closely packed ranks, holding pikes of up to 20 feet long in front of them, these pikemen could easily skewer a stampede of charging knights. The age of the knight had finally come to an end.

Some orders of knighthood which were founded in the Middle Ages still exist today. The Order of the Garter is one of them. ▼

29

Glossary

Aristocrat — a member of the nobility or a privileged class.

Astronomy — the study of stars, planets, comets, etc.

Battering ram — a tree trunk or giant wooden pole, often fitted with an iron tip, which was swung back and forth against a castle wall or gate to smash it down.

Battlement — a line of notches along the top of a wall or tower. Soldiers leaned over the gaps, called crenels, to fire at the enemy below, and took cover behind the higher parts of the wall, called merlons.

Crusades — or wars of the cross, were religious wars, fought by Christians, to win back the Holy Land from the Muslims.

Curtain wall — the wall around a castle.

Faith — religious belief.

Fortress — a place built to resist attack.

Gatehouse — a tower built over a castle's main gates. The gatehouse was the best defended part of a castle.

Holy Land — modern-day Israel, Jordan, Lebanon and Syria. This is the part of the world where Jesus lived and taught.

Lance — long, tapering wooden pole with a metal tip. After about 1100, it became common for knights to charge at their enemy with a lance gripped rigidly under their right armpit.

Longbow — a wooden bow, about the same height as a man.

Moat — a deep trench that was dug around a castle and filled with water.

Muslim — someone who follows the Islamic religion.

Orders — communities of monks or nuns who follow a strict religious way of life. The Templars, the Knights of St. John, and the Teutonic Knights were military orders whose members were supposed to live like monks.

Orders of Knighthood (Orders of Chivalry) — There have been many orders of Knighthood set up over the centuries. Although they may have started up for different reasons, each order was like an exclusive knight club. Members promised to support one another at all times, to obey their Master and to do knightly deeds. Unlike monastic orders, such as the Templars, these orders of Knighthood did not vow to live like monks.

Page — child being trained for the rank of knight.

Poleaxe — a battle-ax with a heavy head ("poll"), set on a four to six foot wooden pole.

Rampart — a wall-like barrier.

Ransom — goods or money demanded for the release of a prisoner.

Squire — a trainee knight.

Vow — a solemn promise.

RESOURCES

BOOKS TO READ

Knights by Carole Corbin (New York: Franklin Watts, 1989)

Knights and Castles by Jonathan Rutland (New York: Random House, 1987)

Knights of the Round Table by Gwen Gross (New York: Random House, 1985)

The Medieval Knight by Martin Windrow (New York: Franklin Watts, 1985)

Castles by Richard Clarke (New York: Bookwright, 1986)

Castles and Crusaders by Philip Sauvain (New York: Warwick, 1986)

Chivalry and the Mailed Knight by Walter Buehr (New York: Putnam, 1963)

A COLORING BOOK

Knights and Armors Coloring Book by A. G. Smith (New York: Dover, 1985)

VIDEO GAMES

CastleVania (Konami)

Simon's Quest (Konami)

PLACES TO VISIT

Check with local museums in your area to see if they have armor on display, as well as medieval weapons, paintings, and tapestries.

The Metropolitan Museum of Art, The Cloisters, Fort Tryon Park, New York

West Point Museum, United States Military Academy, West Point, New York

INDEX

Additional photographs: Bibliotheque Nationale (243 Fol. 79) 15(b), (2630 Fol. 22V) 20(bl); Bodleian Library (Ms Bodley 264 Fol. 59r) 6(br); British Library (K7853) 12(br), (Ms Harley 4379 Fol 43) cover (bl) and 17(tr); Camera Press 29(br); ET Archive (ref. Ms 244/A) 15(tl), 28(tr); Chris Fairclough Colour Library (Ashley Holding) 7(tr), (Sylvia Kelly) 23(br), (Stephen Crispe) 24(bl); Robert Harding Picture Library 21(b); Pierpont Morgan Library (Stavelot Triptoh) 4(br), (M638 f23v) 8(t), (M775 122v) 10(tr); Cadw Welsh Historic Monuments 13(tl).